FUNNY AND USEFUL BRITISH INSULTS COLORING BOOK

This coloring book is designed to relieve stress by having a laugh and learning some british insults that may come in useful when addressing the annoying people in our life.

The coloring pages vary to cater for beginners and more advanced colorists. Each design is blank at the back to avoid bleed through.

Have fun and don't let those bastards get you down!

Copyright© 2020 Happy Bear Books

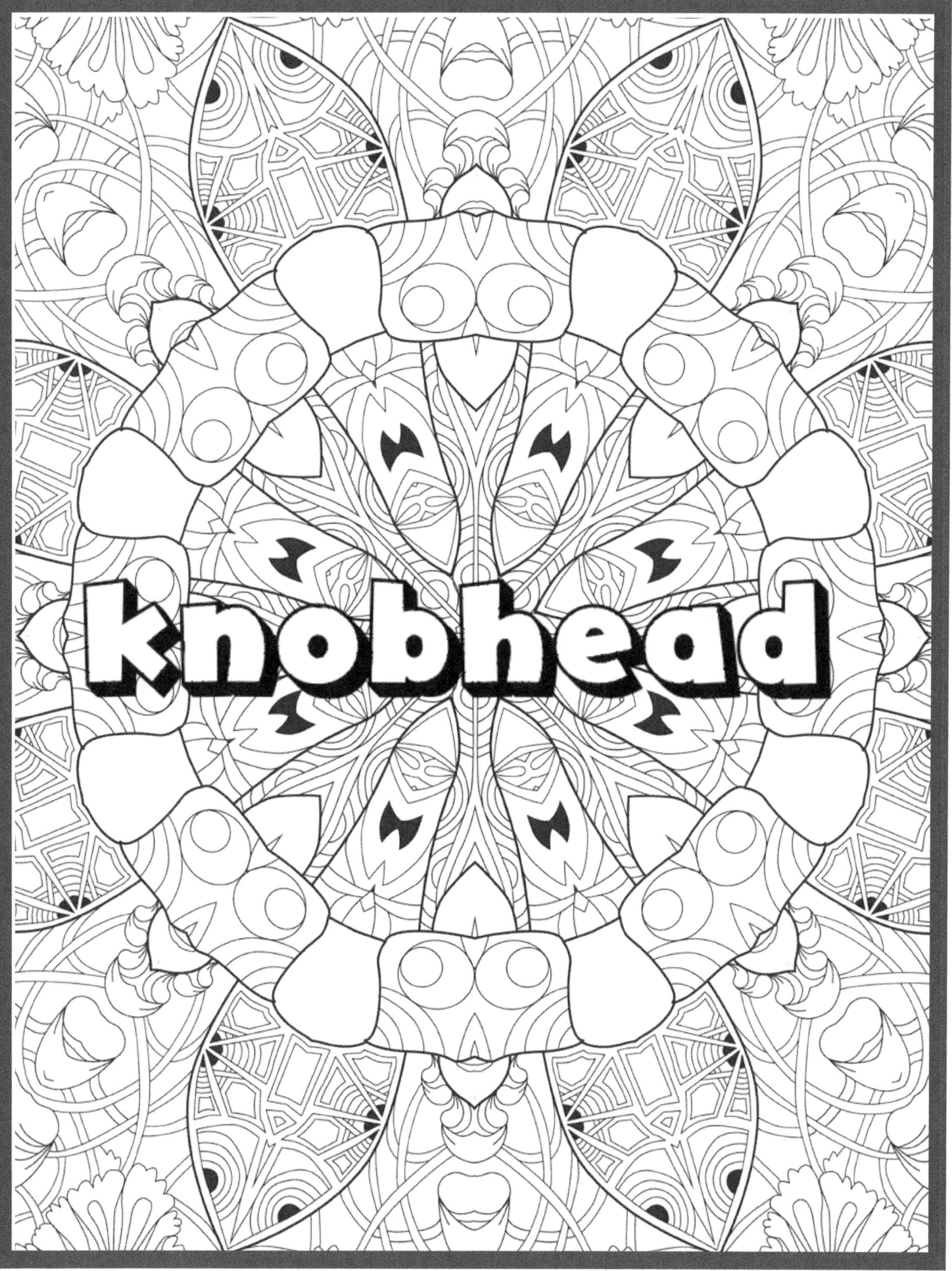

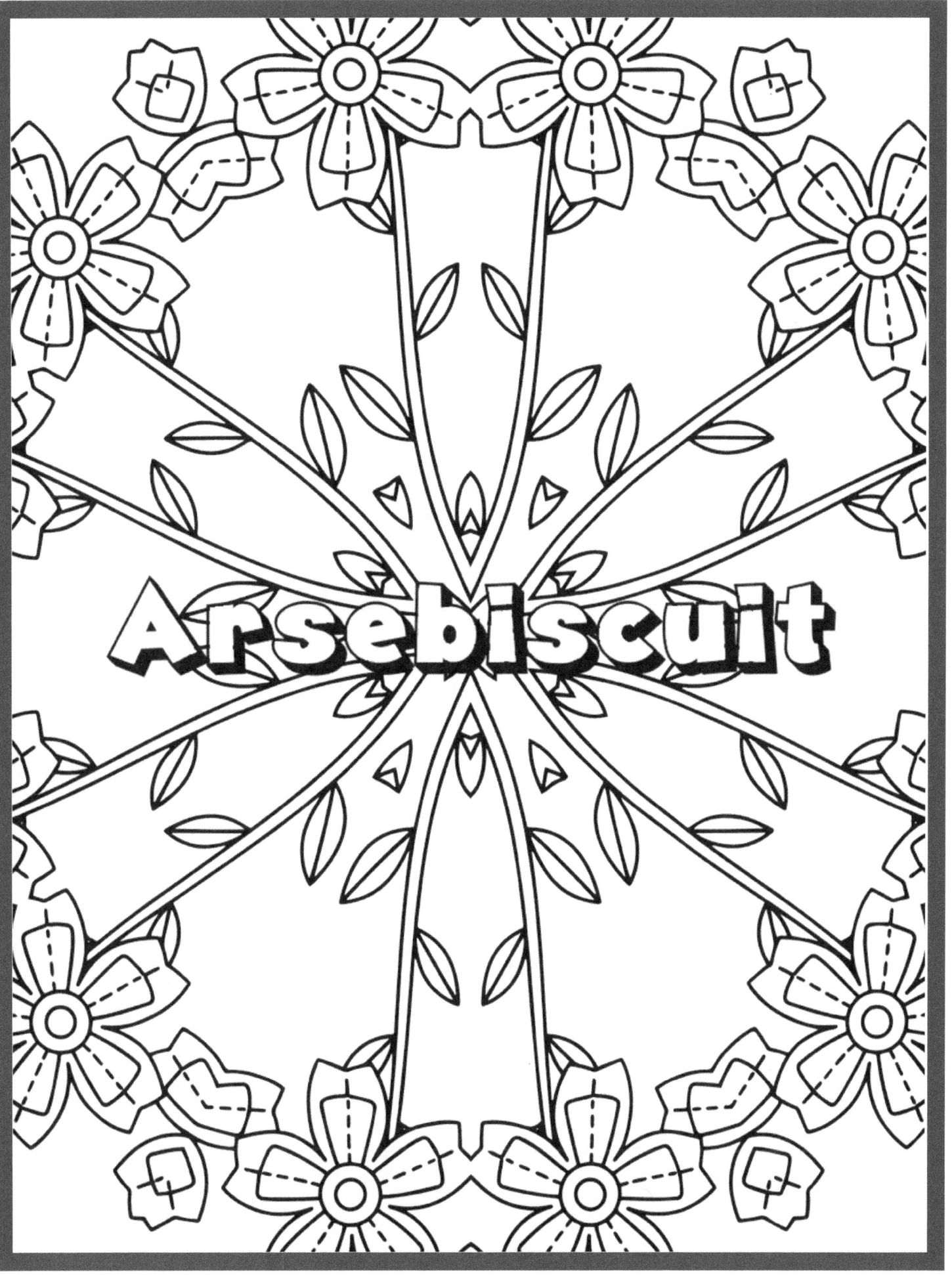

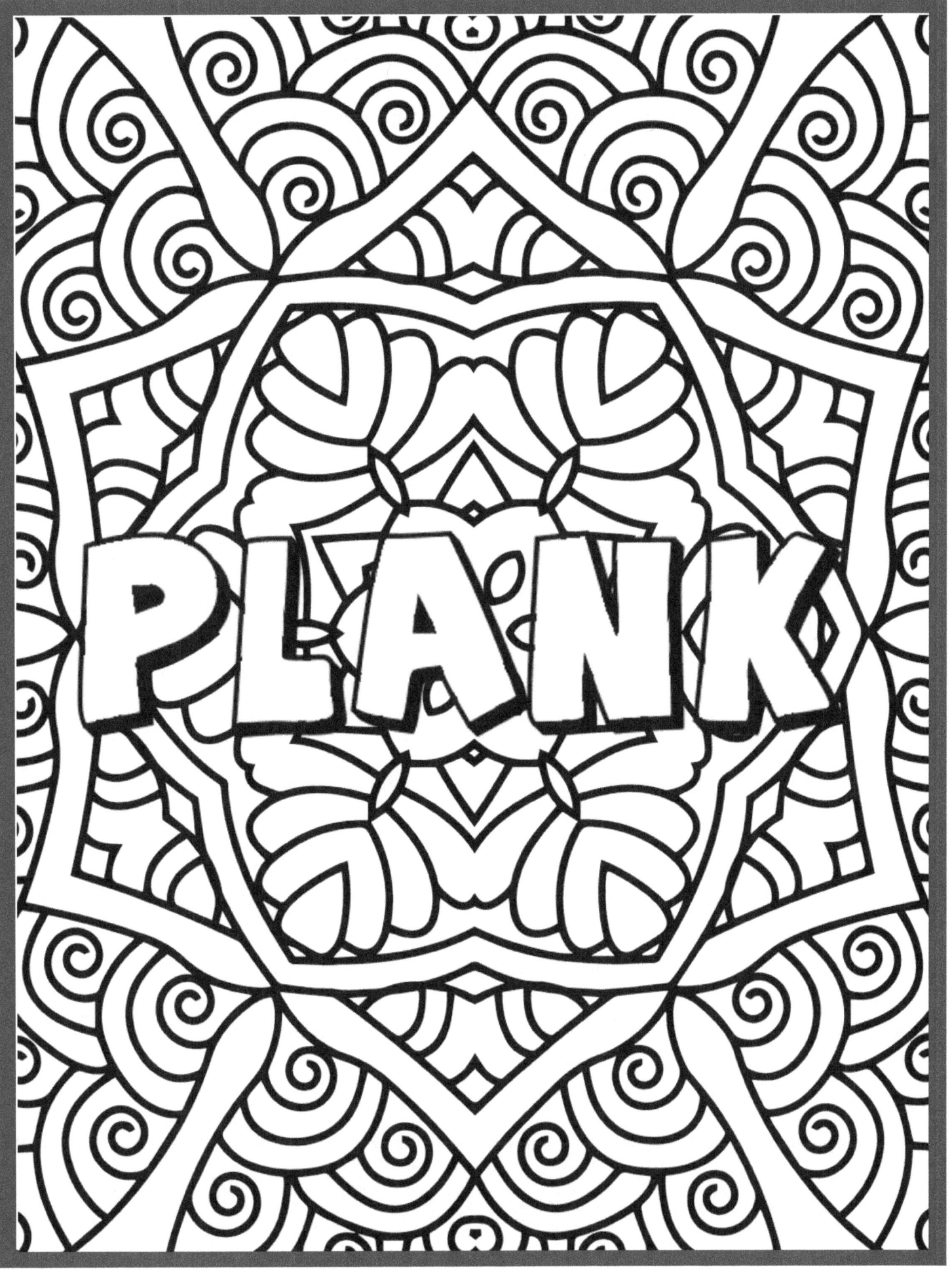

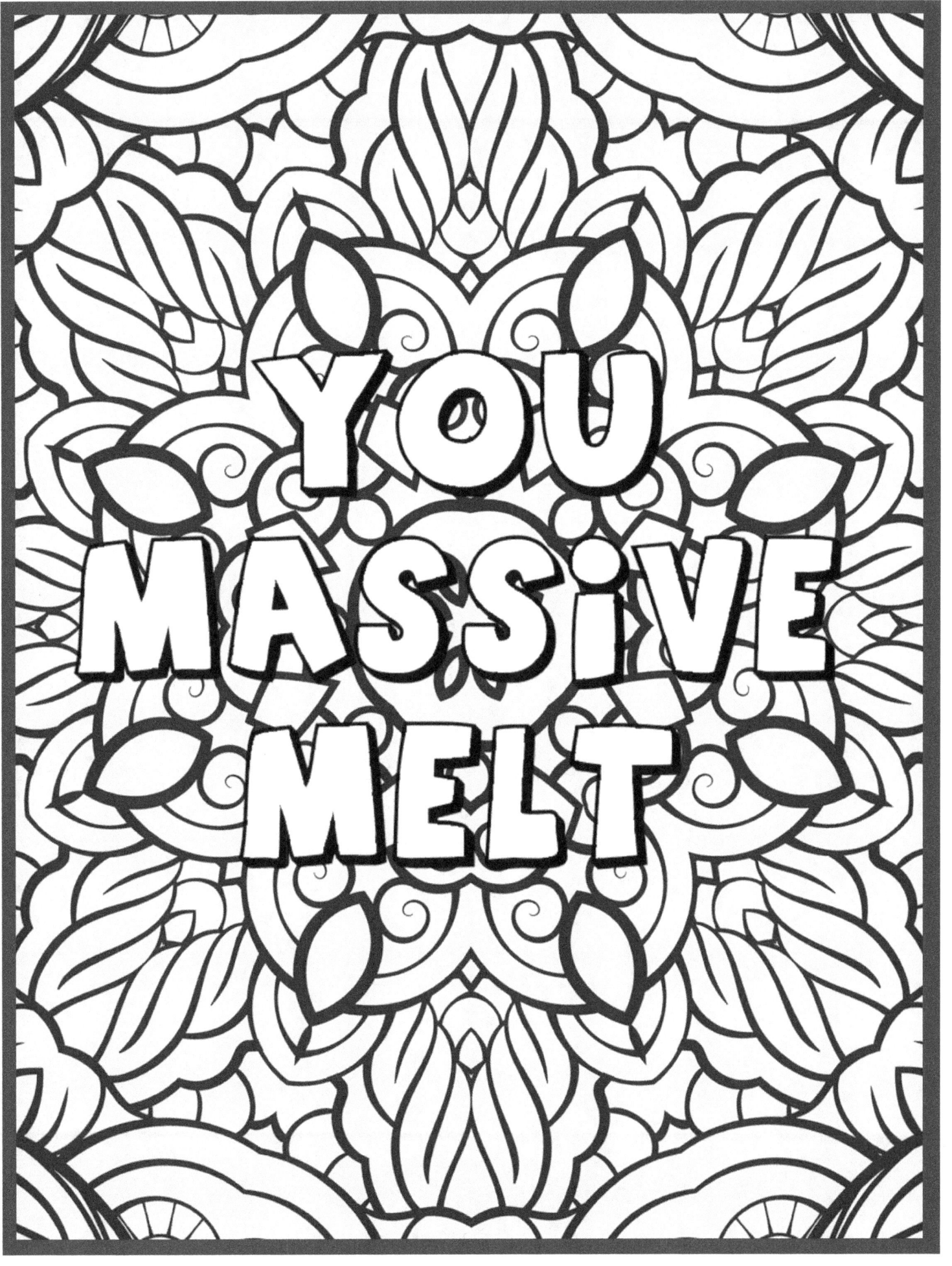

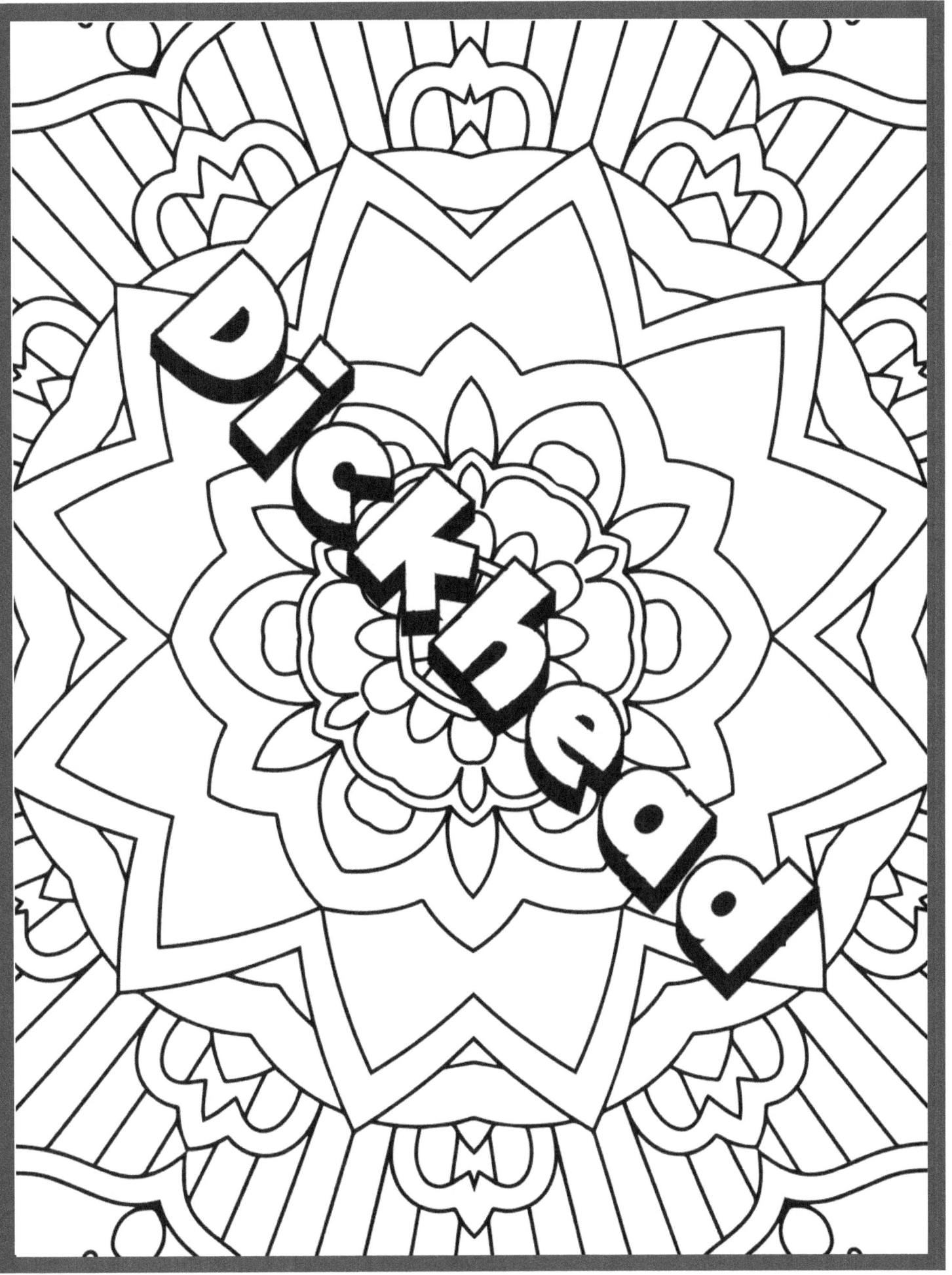

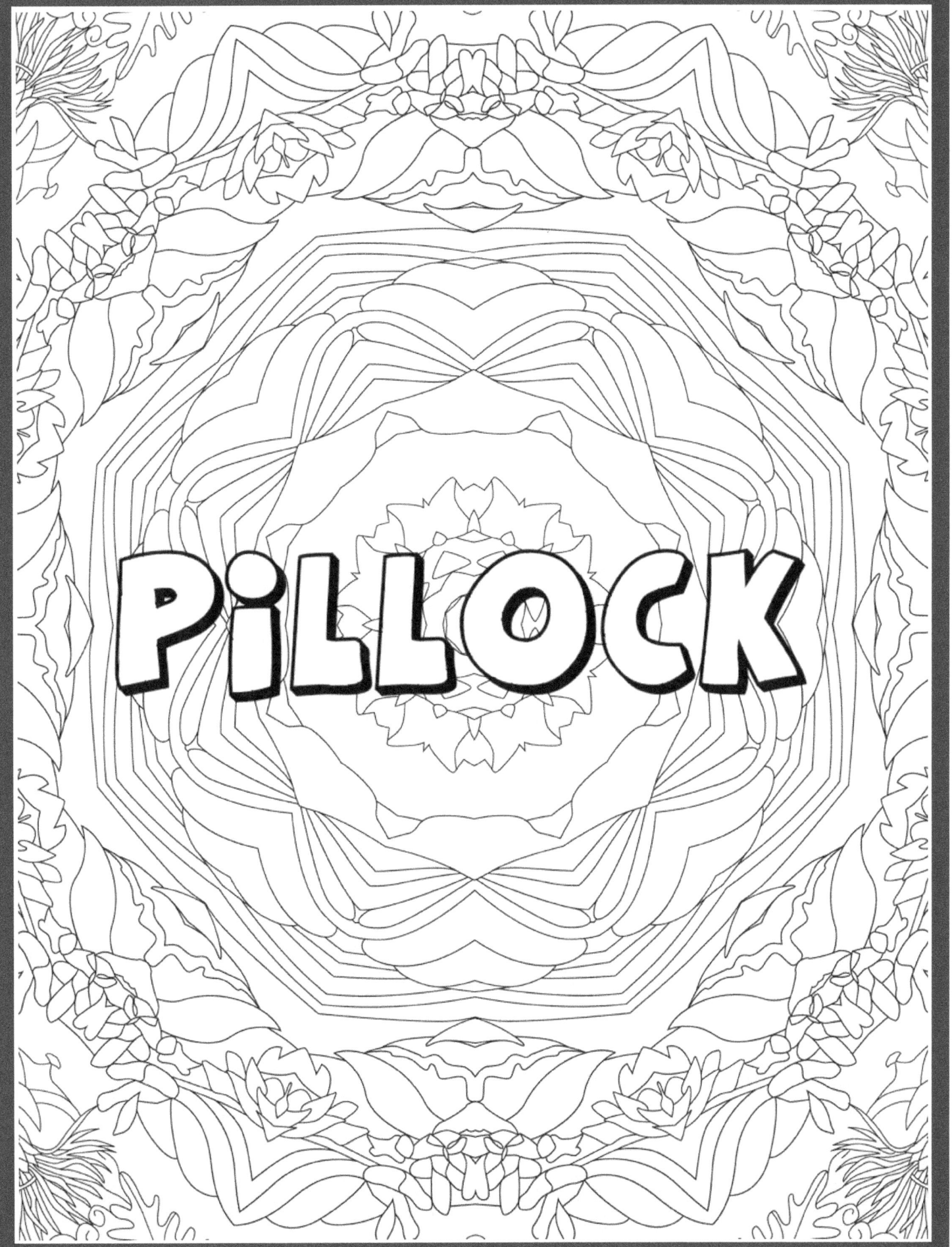

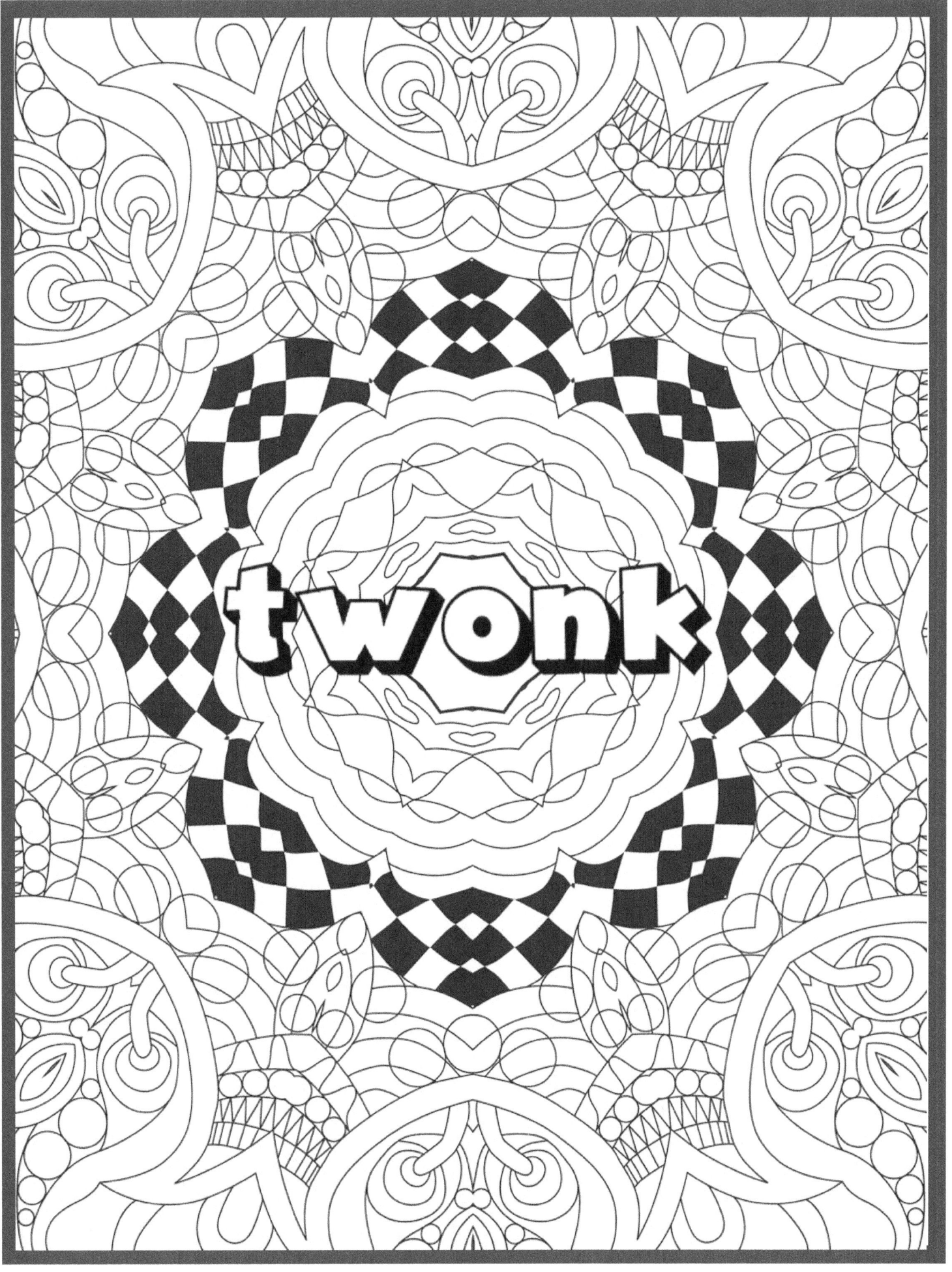

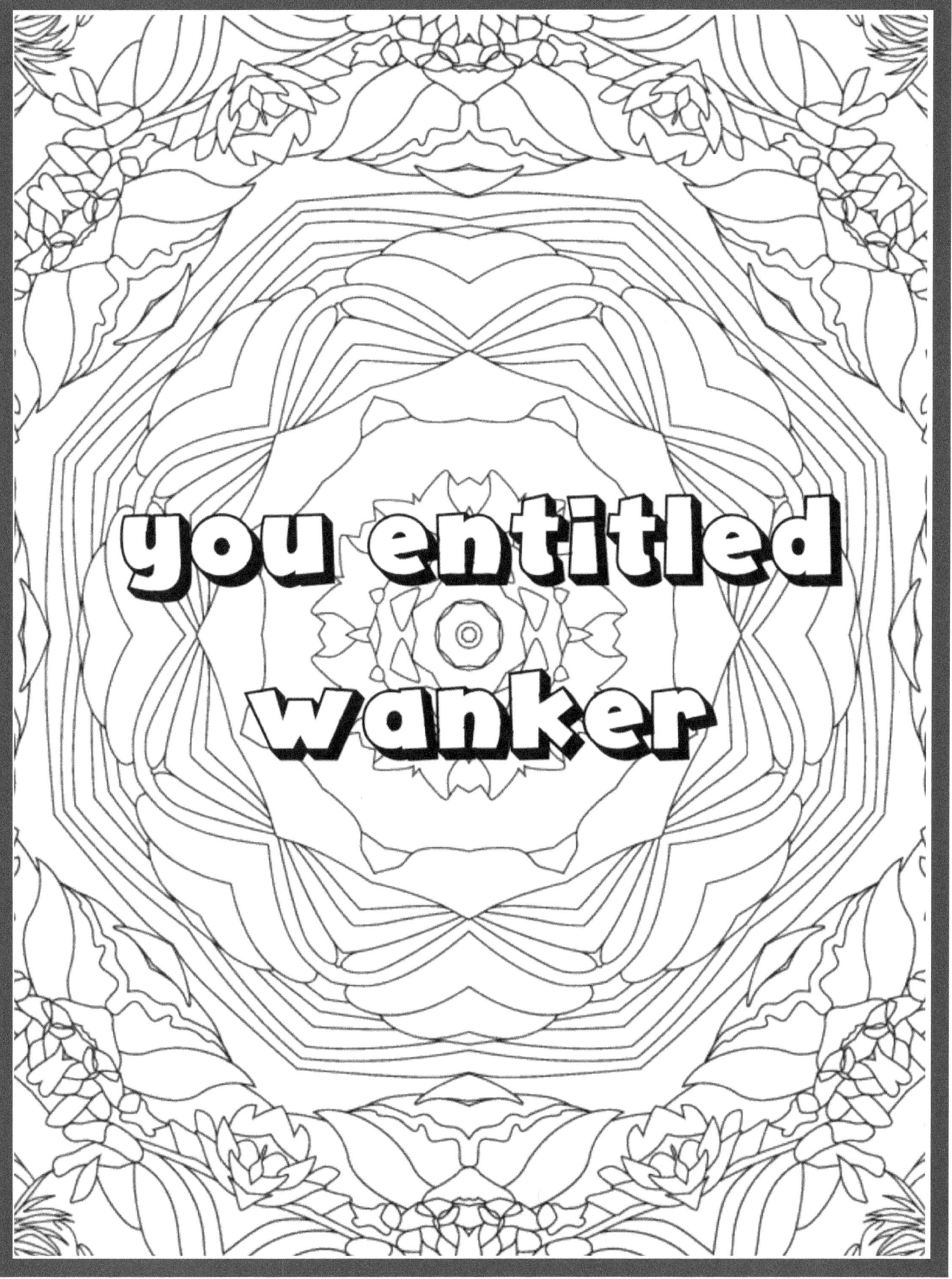

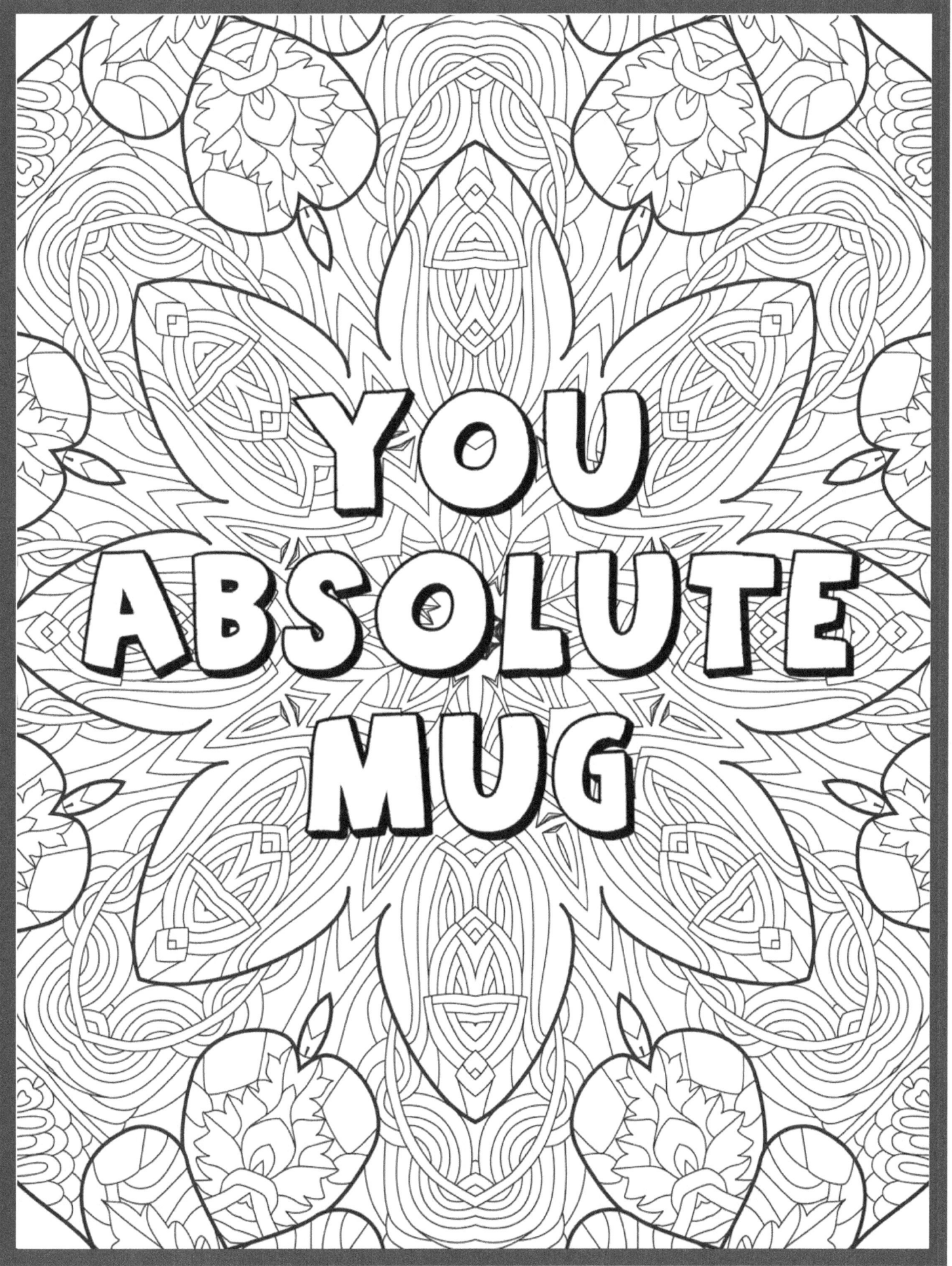

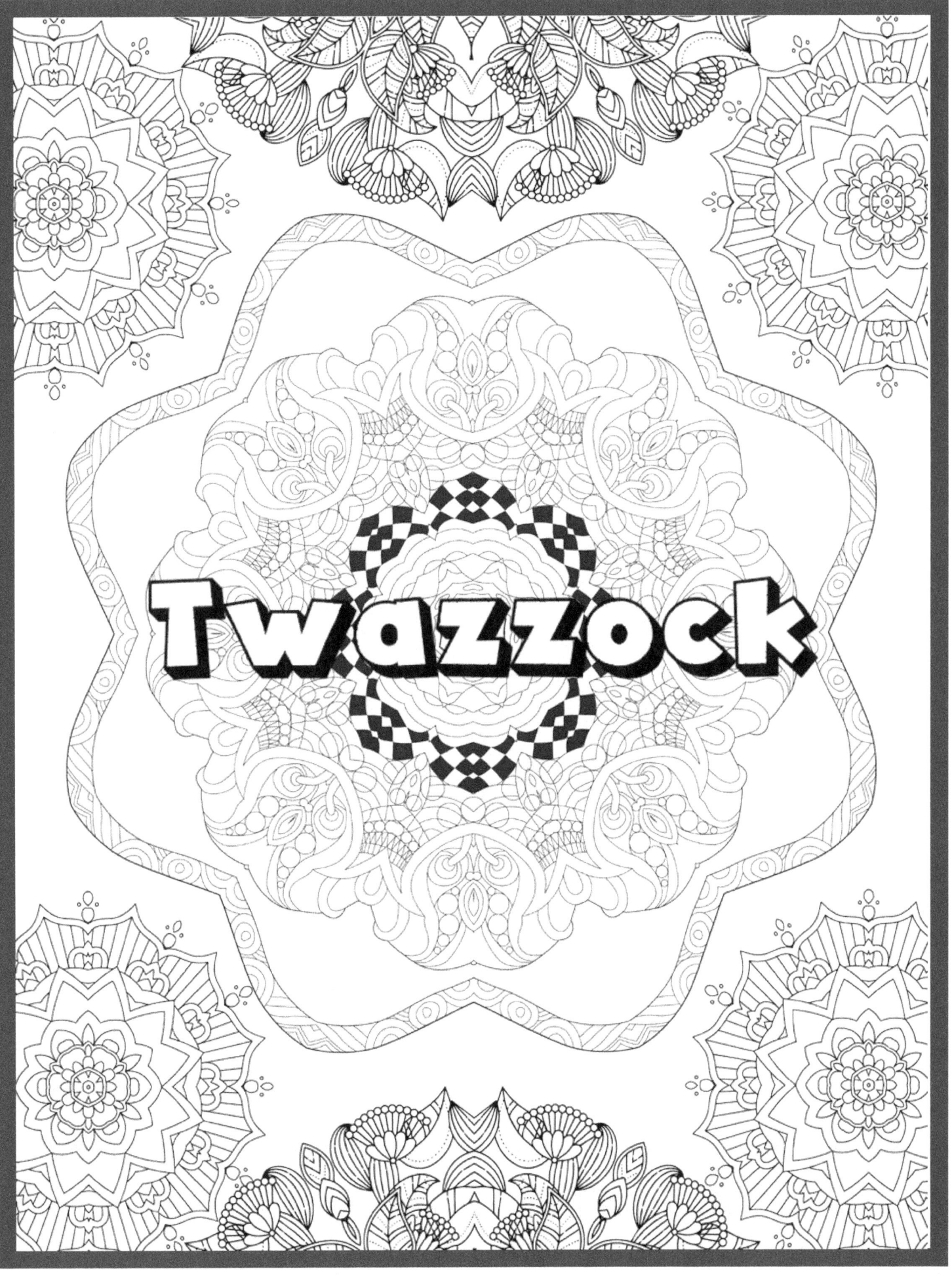

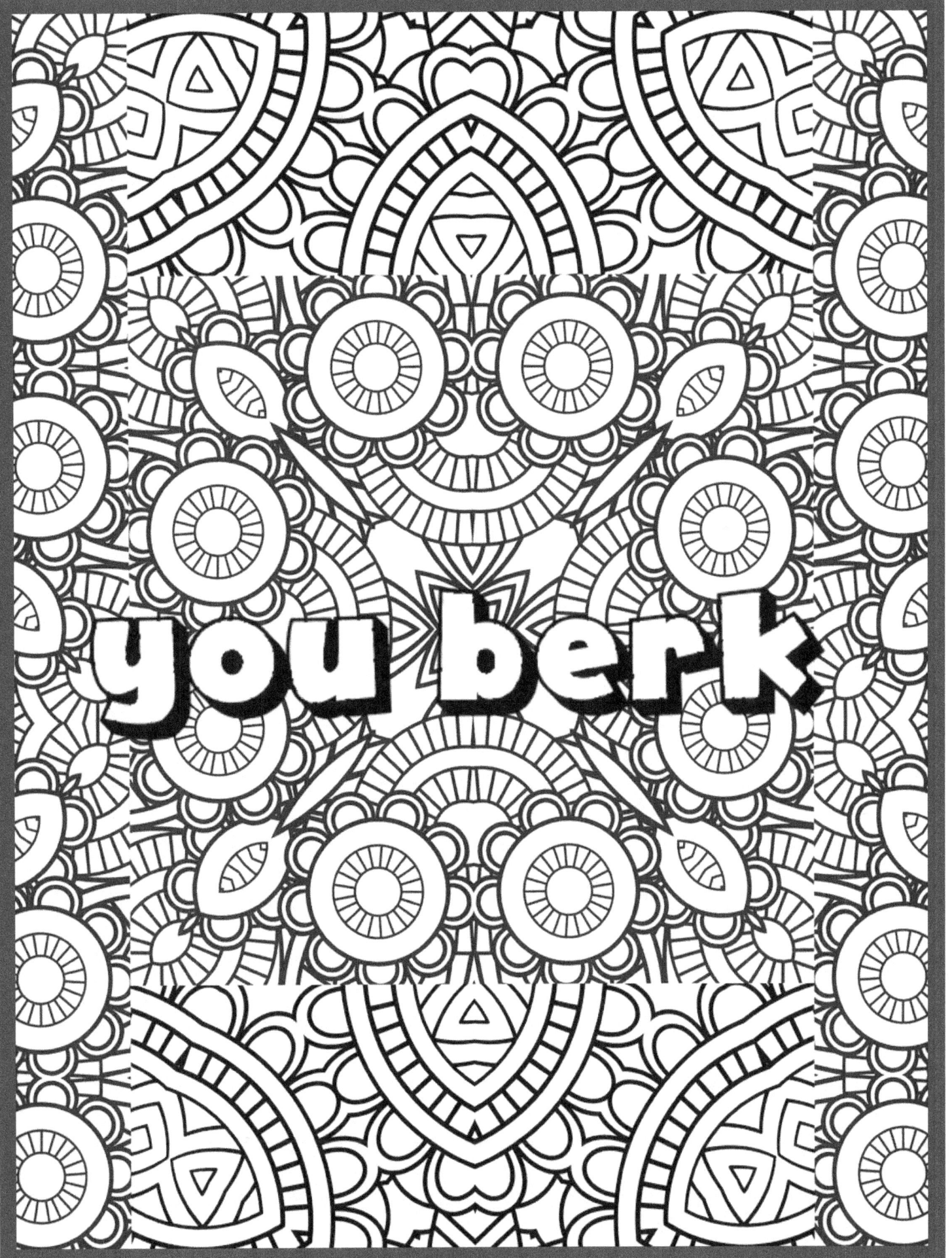

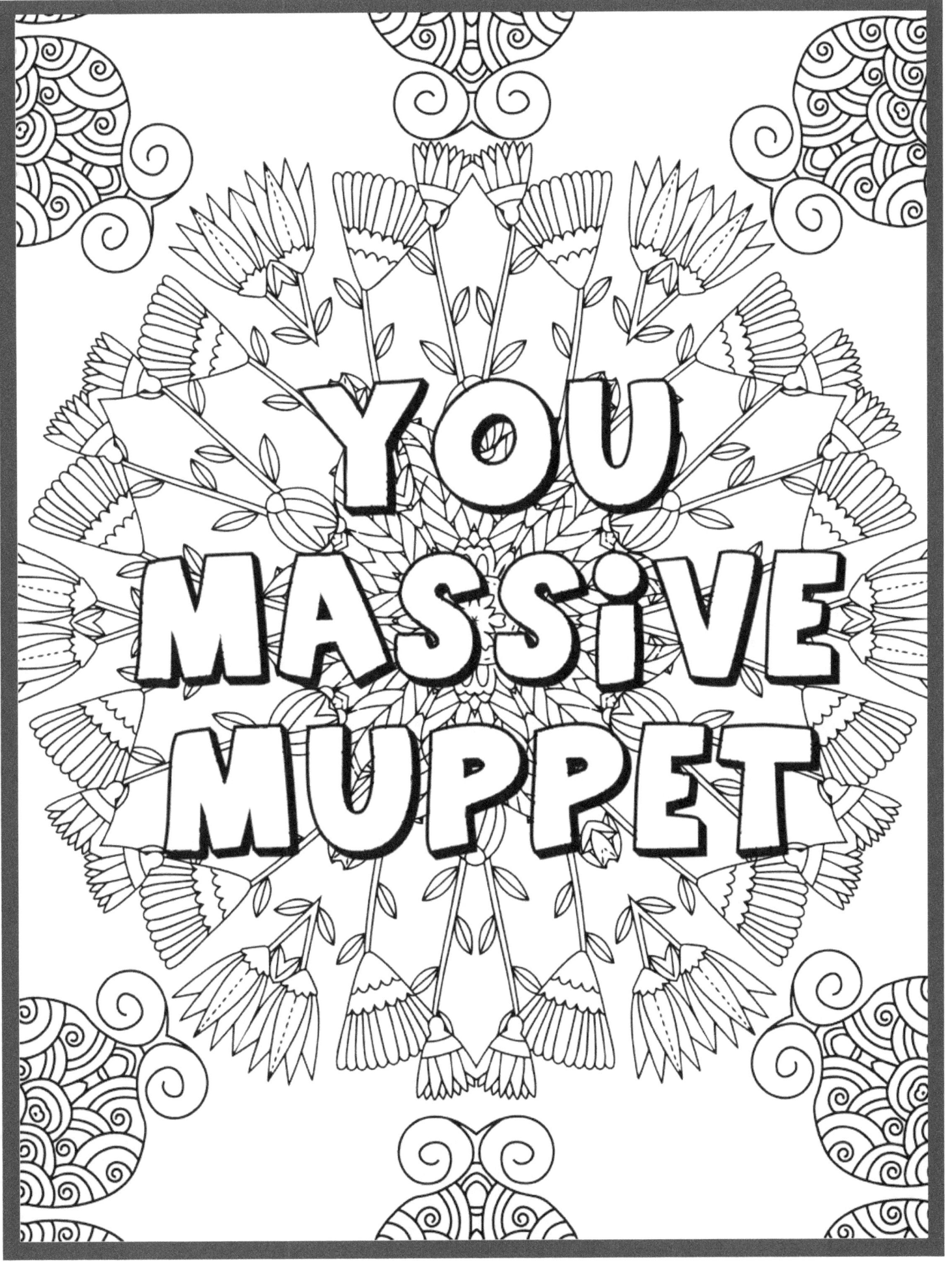

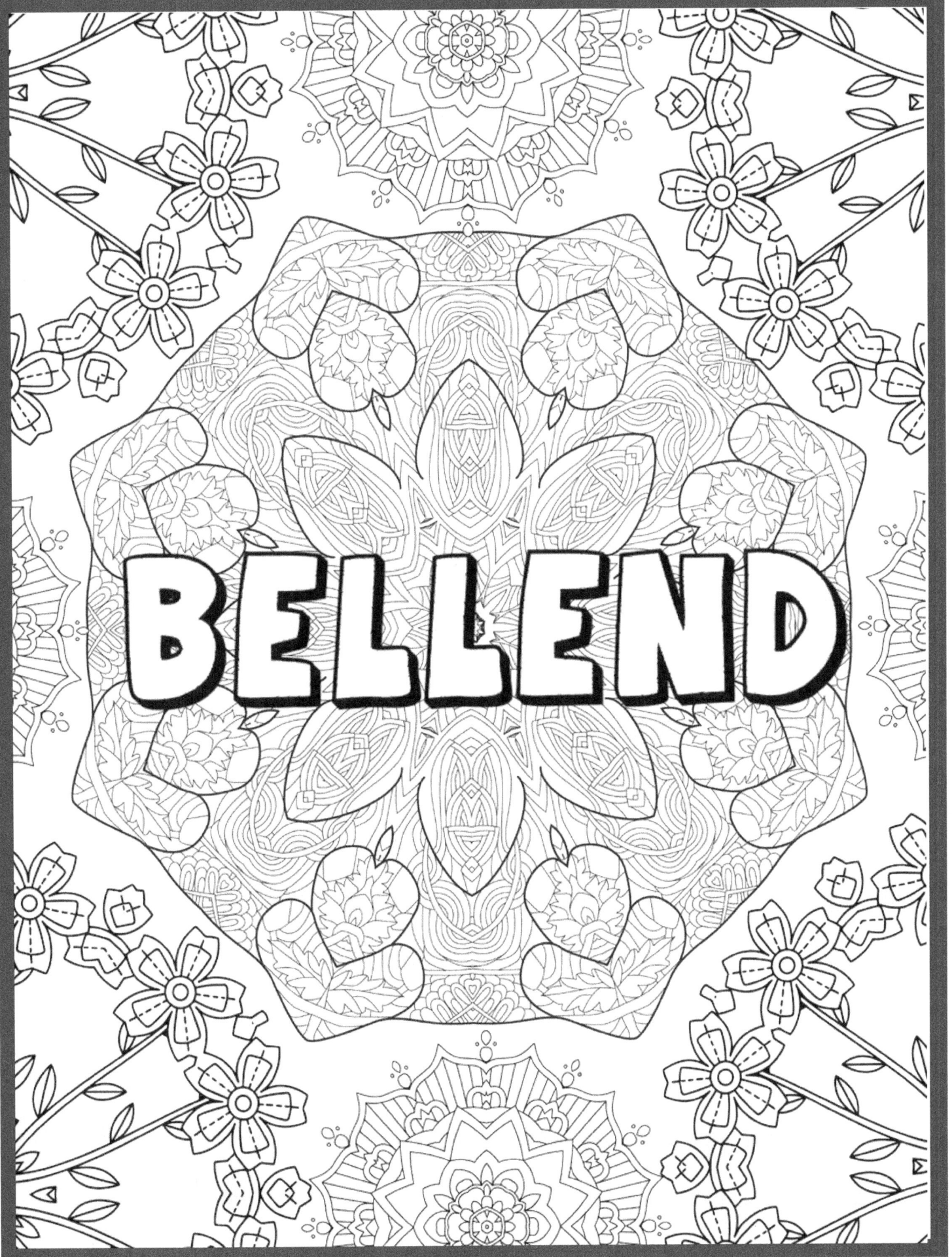

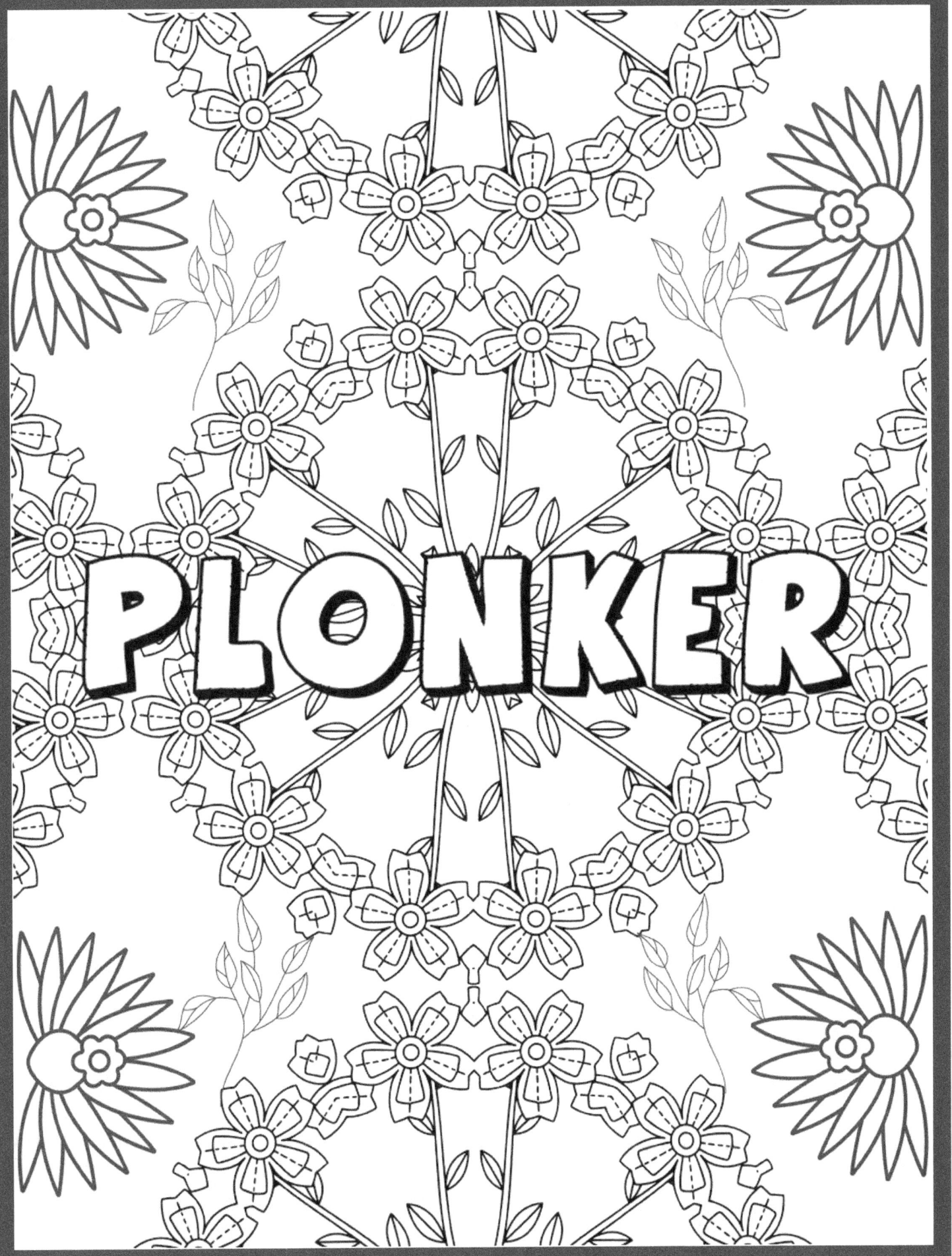

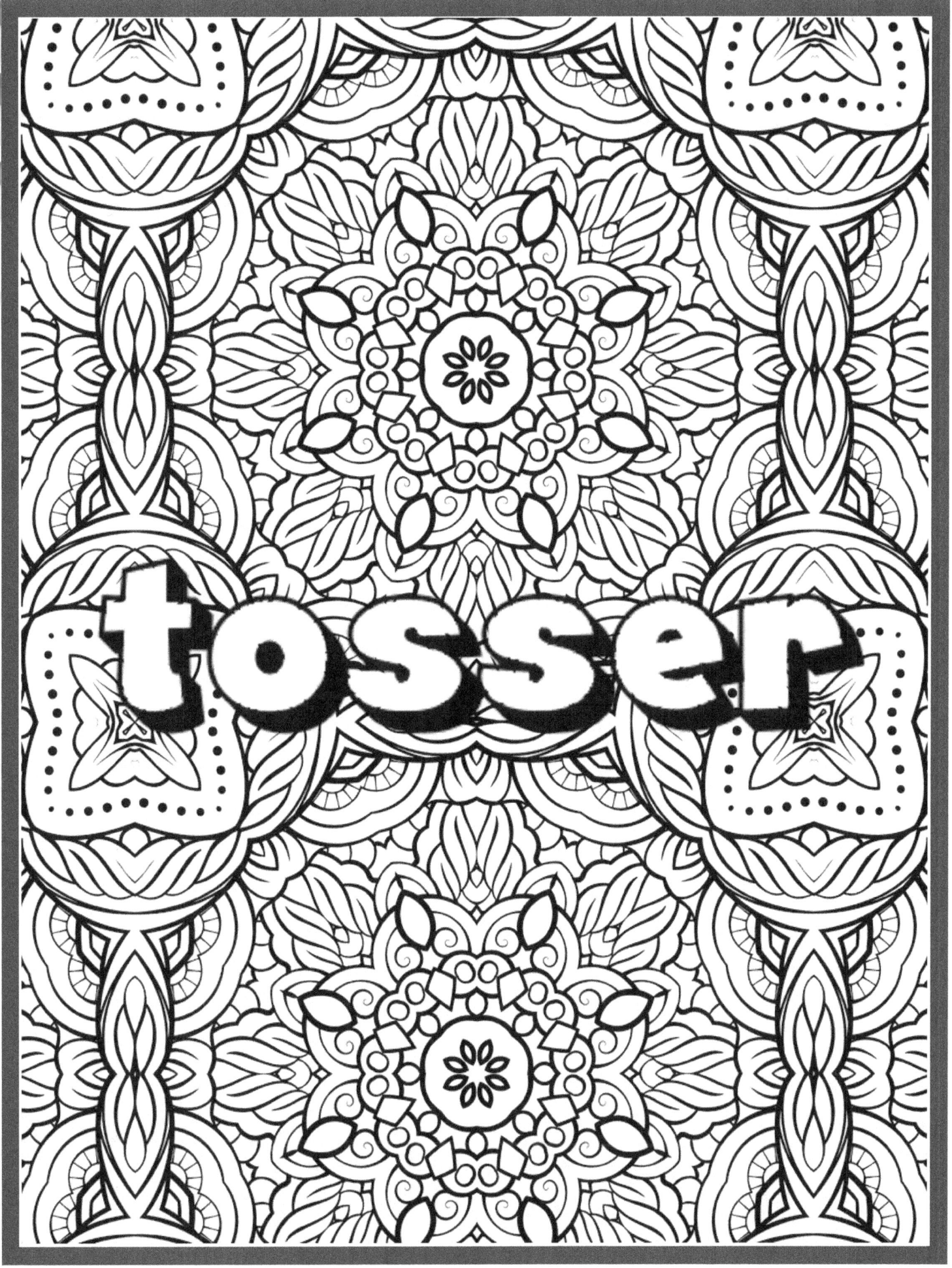

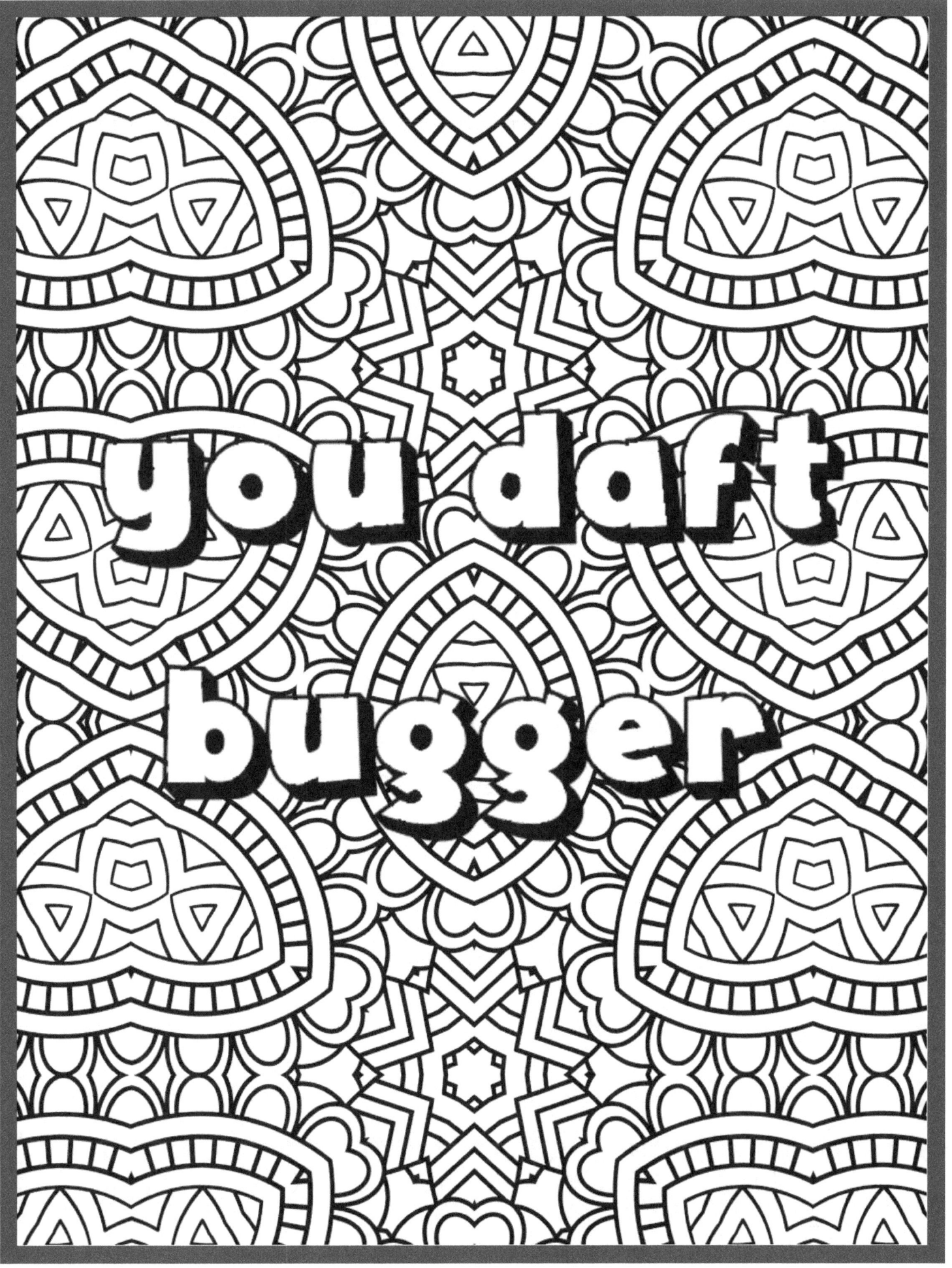

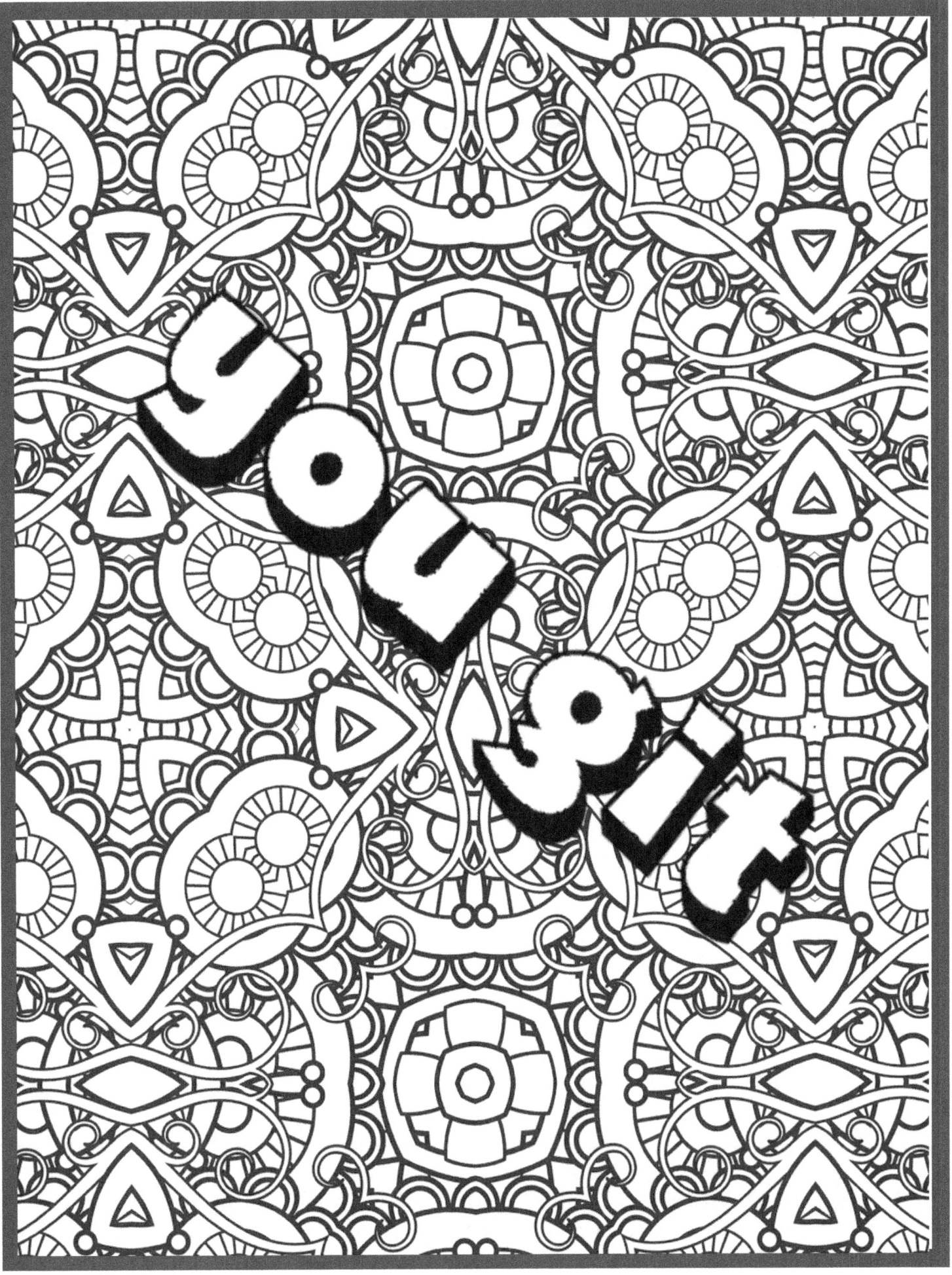

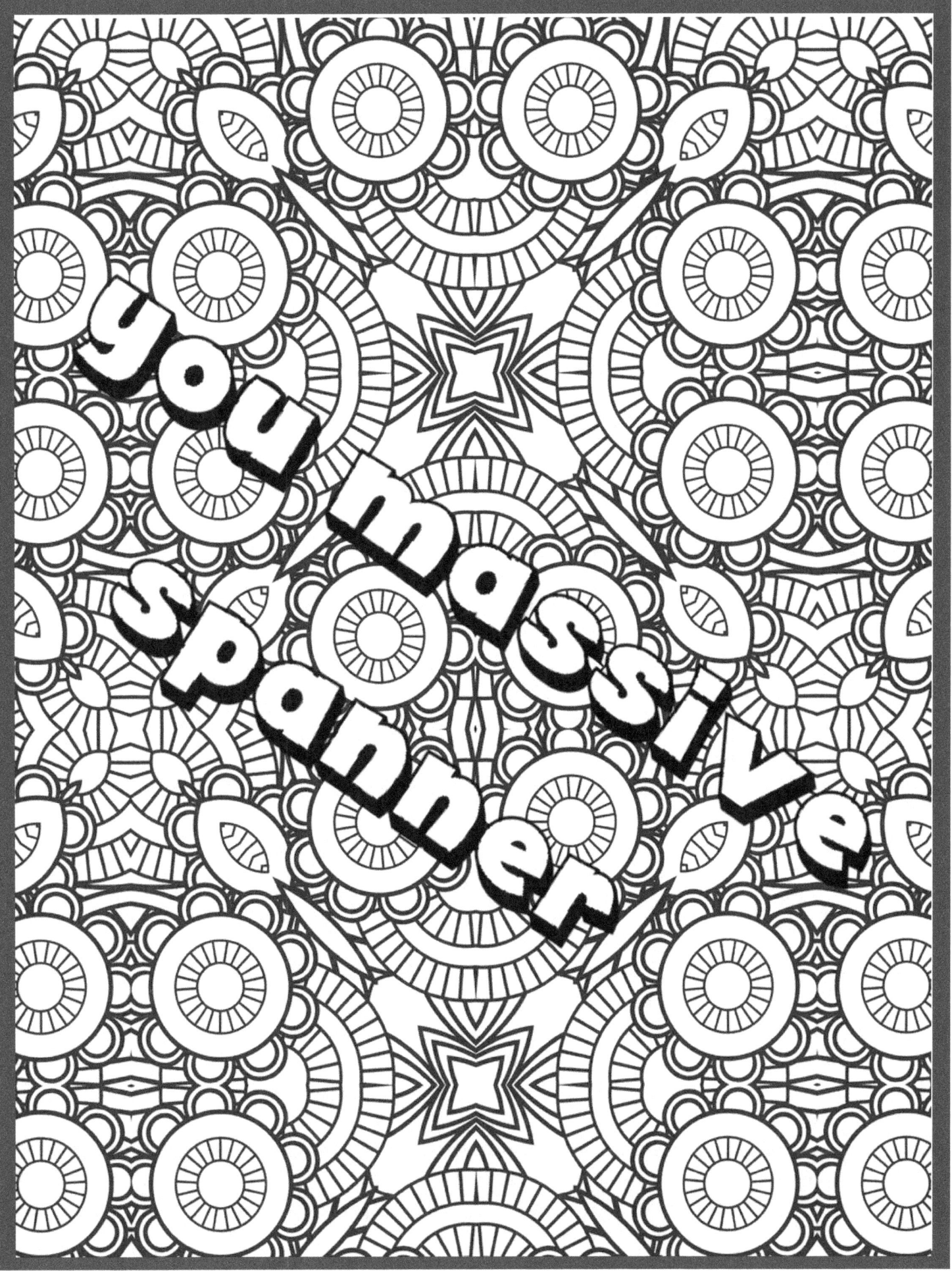

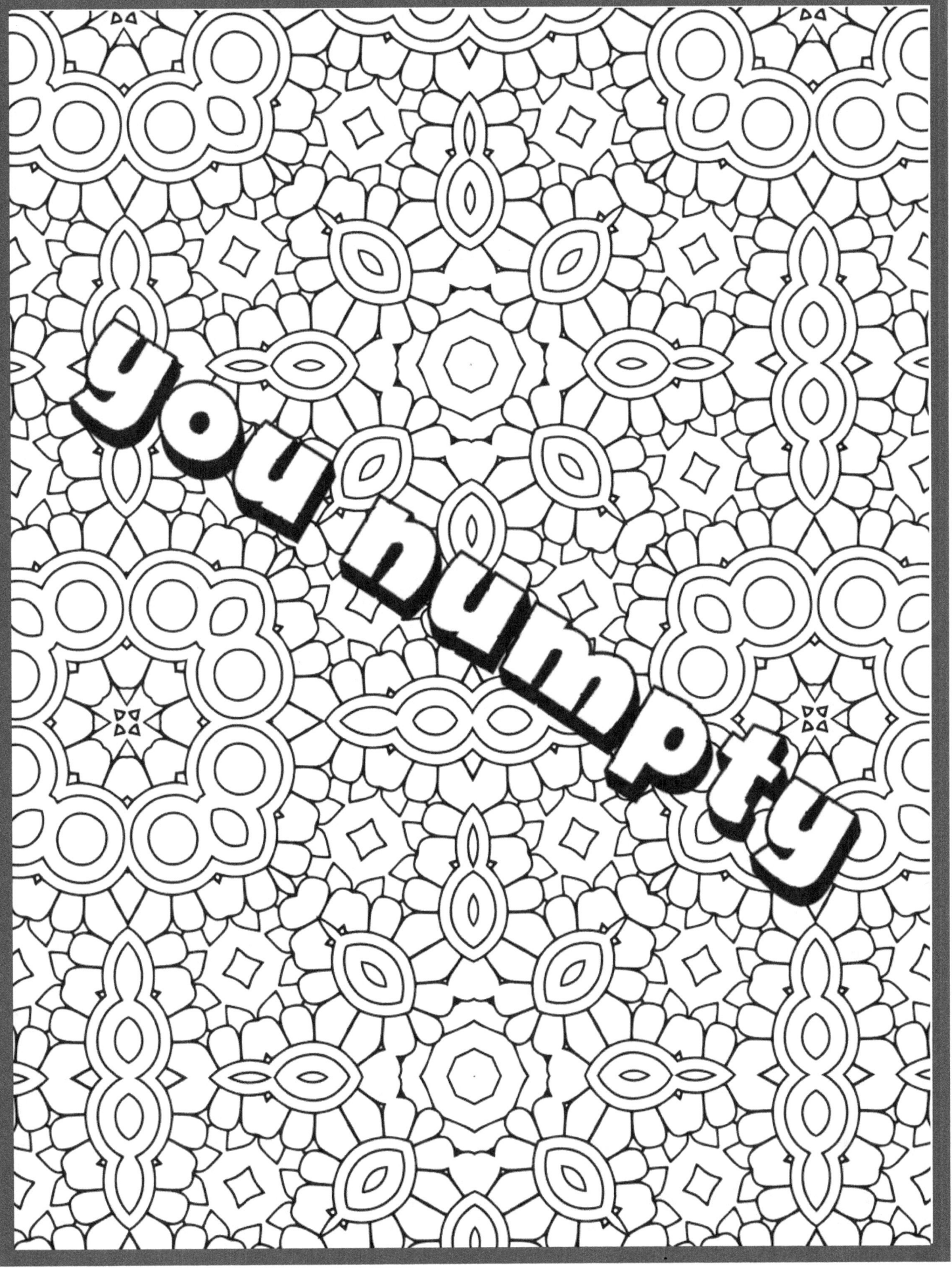

www.ingramcontent.com/pod-product-compliance
Lightning Source LLC
Chambersburg PA
CBHW081753240526
45465CB00033B/3329